To:

From:

Cats @Work ™

by Kathy Weller

PETER PAUPER PRESS, INC.
White Plains, New York

OUR COMPANY

In 1928, at the age of twenty-two, Peter Beilenson began printing books on a small press in the basement of his parents' home in Larchmont, New York. Peter—and later, his wife, Edna—sought to create fine books that sold at "prices even a pauper could afford."

Today, still family owned and operated, Peter Pauper Press continues to honor our founders' legacy—and our customers' expectations—of beauty, quality, and value.

———————

I dedicate this book to the Cats@Work™ social media community.
*They keep ME laughing, too—all day, every day, not just Monday through Friday! ^__^*

-Kathy

Text and illustrations copyright ©2015 Kathy Weller Art + Ideas www.kathyweller.com

Published by
Peter Pauper Press, Inc.
202 Mamaroneck Avenue
White Plains, NY 10601

ISBN 978-1-4413-1843-5
Printed in China
7 6 5 4 3 2 1

Visit us at www.peterpauper.com

cats@work™

by Kathy Weller

CONTENTS

Cats@Work™ began as a way for me to find humor in the follies of my day job. What started as my own personal coping mechanism grew into a five-day-a-week comic on social media. Pretty soon, people were discovering Cats@Work™, LOL'ing to it with their morning coffee, and sharing it with their friends. With comments such as "This is ME!" or "This is YOU!" it became clear to me that most everyone could relate to Cats@Work™ in some way, whether they worked in an office or not.

If you can't function without your morning coffee, if your co-workers drive you nuts, or if deadlines rule your life, Cats@Work™ is for you. More than just a comic—it's therapy! The snarky humor paired with these brassy cats encourages ALL of us to look on the bright side of each workday—and to laugh at ourselves in the process. I hope that Cats@Work™ adds a jolt of catty office humor and dry wit to your daily grind EVERY day, not just Monday through Friday. You should DEFINITELY laugh at your job, and Cats@Work™ gives you permission to do so! (Just keep it hidden from your boss!) ^_ ^

Kathy

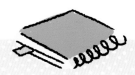

AND SO IT BEGINS

IT'S MONDAY.

LET'S DO THIS.

IT'S TUESDAY.

JUST DON'T EXPECT GENUINE ENTHUSIASM.

WEDNESDAY.

SOME CALL IT HUMP DAY.

I CALL IT GRUMP DAY.

Every Second Counts

I DON'T HAVE A
time-management
PROBLEM.

It's only a problem for everyone else.

IT'S REALLY IMPORTANT TO NEVER BE LATE

WHEN YOU'RE BEING WATCHED

I ONLY HIT SNOOZE TWICE TODAY.

I DESERVE A MEDAL.

TIME FOR A BATHROOM BREAK

...SO I CAN READ MY PHONE IN PEACE

Late Again.

because
looking
this good
takes
time.

APPTS.

THREE HOURS' TRAINING.

ZERO RETENTION.

(AWESOME NAP.)

HOLD EVERYTHING.

IT's TIME for my COOKIE.

I MUST BE IN A
TIME WARP

BECAUSE THIS DAY IS SIX MONTHS LONG.

DEPARTURE TIME "SAFE ZONE"
rapidly approaching

EMPLOYEE
OF THE
MONTH

30

33

THEY DON'T PAY ME

FOR MY SPARKLING PERSONALITY.

DON'T LOOK SO SURPRISED.

34

JUST DON'T EXPECT TOO MUCH

AND YOU WON'T BE DISAPPOINTED ☺

IT'S HARD WORK LOOKING THIS BUSY

I CAN'T COMPLAIN ABOUT MY JOB
if you won't listen

Just deal
with it

41

42

THIS PROJECT is

EATING MY BRAIN

WHY

DO I WORK HERE, AGAIN?

47

PLEASE COME BACK IN FIVE MINUTES

FIVE HOURS, EIGHT DAYS, AND THREE MONTHS.

K Thanks!

YES YOU CAN!

TROPICAL
DESKTOP WALLPAPERS

ARE
SO,
SO
MEAN.

MY TO-DO LIST

HAS A TO-DO LIST

AT SOME POINT,

THIS MADE PERFECT SENSE.

YOU THINK YOU'RE BUSY?

THINK AGAIN.

Enter ENTHUSED

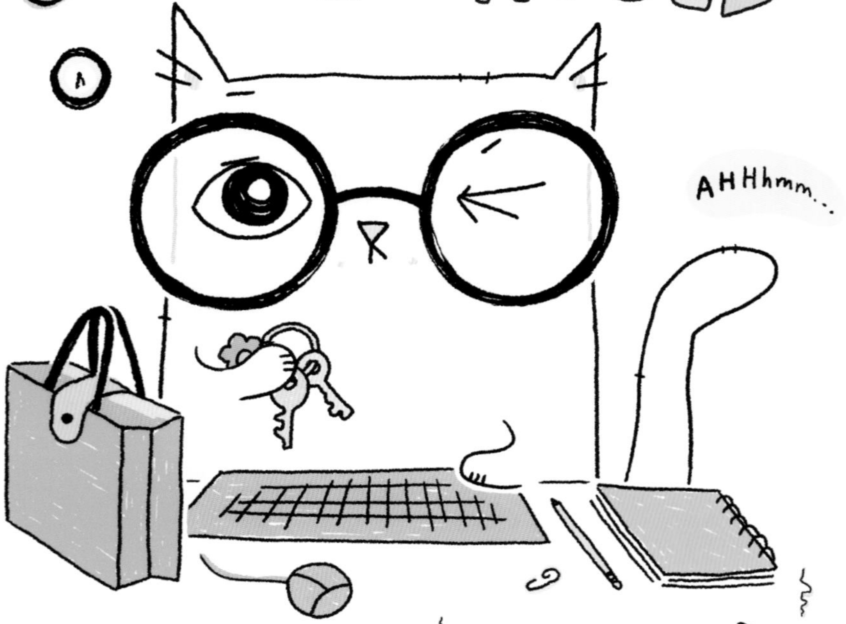

Exit CONFUSED

I.T. MATTERS

HEADPHONES

make me nicer

oh, Hello there.

It was just writing you a scathing email.

Dear Technology,

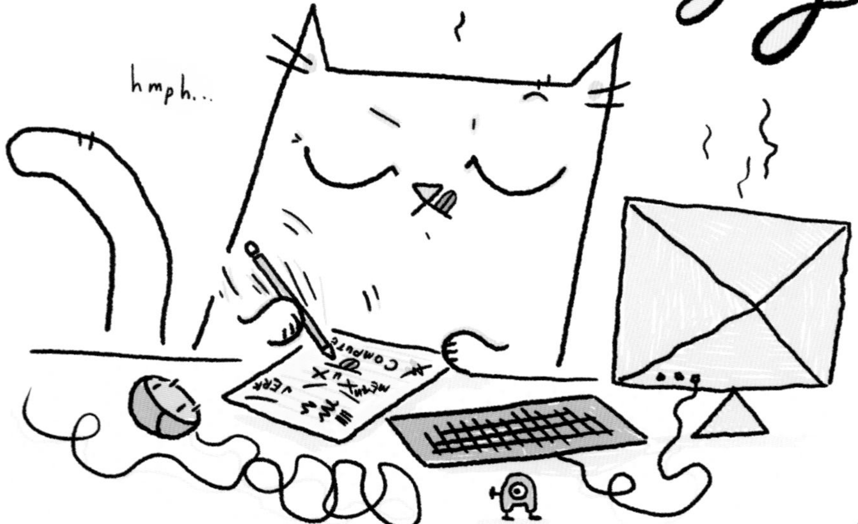

You are being a jerk.

Catty Politics

Be nice to me today.

you might need something tomorrow.

69

SMILE

IF YOU HAVE SOMETHING ON YOUR BOSS

I'm not above a little bribery

Being SUPER-POLITE freaks people out.

Congratulations!
You Win
JUST FOR YOU
the "Most Obnoxious Co-Worker" Award

SNARKY SERVICE

SORRY, BUT I CAN'T HEAR YOU OVER THE CONFERENCE CALL IN MY HEAD

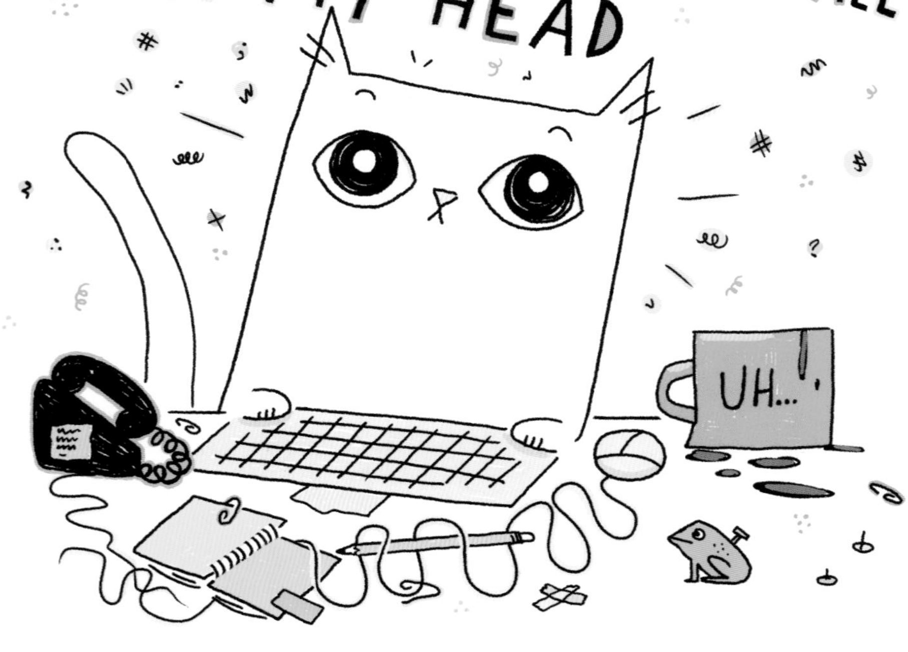

87

89

I LIKE THE WORD PLEASE.

it softens the blow.

YOU CAN DO IT

HAVING A RESPECTABLE, WELL-PAYING JOB

ALLOWS ME TO AFFORD THE THINGS THAT REALLY MATTER.

Life is but a dream

(before 9, after 5, and on weekends)

IT MAY NOT BE
FUN
CHART OF UGH
JUST SHOW UP
OH BOY
BUT IT NEEDS TO GET DONE

The Help Desk

MODEL EMPLOYEES

RARELY MAKE HISTORY

109

COUNT TO TEN

AND WATCH BABY PANDAS.